HARD
TIMES
COME
AGAIN
NO MORE

HARD TIMES COME AGAIN NO MORE

Suffering and Hope

ALEX JOYNER

Abingdon Press / Nashville

HARD TIMES COME AGAIN NO MORE
SUFFERING AND HOPE

Copyright © 2010 by Abingdon Press

This book is printed on acid-free paper.

Library of Congress Cataloging-in-Publication Data

Joyner, Alex.
   Hard times come again no more : suffering and hope / Alex Joyner.
    p cm.
   Includes bibligraphical references and index.
   ISBN 978-1-4267-0370-6 (book - paperback/trade pbk. adhesive,
perfect bindfing : alk papr) 1. Consolation. 2. Suffering—
Religious aspects—Christianity. I. Title.
   BV4905.3.J69   2010
   248.8'6—dc22

                     2010023702

10 11 12 13 14 15 16 17 18 19—10 9 8 7 6 5 4 3 2 1

MANUFACTURED IN THE UNITED STATES OF AMERICA

To the memory of Barbara Tankard

Hard Times Come Again No More

Stephen Collins Foster

Let us pause in life's pleasures and count its many tears,
While we all sup sorrow with the poor;
There's a song that will linger forever in our ears;
Oh! Hard Times, come again no more.

Chorus
'Tis the song, the sigh of the weary,
Hard Times, Hard Times, come again no more:
Many days you have lingered around my cabin door;
Oh! Hard Times, come again no more.

While we seek mirth and beauty and music light and gay,
There are frail forms fainting at the door;
Tho' their voices are silent, their pleading looks will say
Oh! Hard Times, come again no more.

There's a pale drooping maiden who toils her life away,
With a worn heart whose better days are o'er:
Though her voice would be merry, 'tis sighing all the day,
Oh! Hard Times, come again no more.

'Tis a sigh that is wafted across the troubled wave,
'Tis a wail that is heard upon the shore,
'Tis a dirge that is murmured around the lowly grave,
Oh! Hard Times, come again no more.

—*The Melodies of Stephen C. Foster* (Pittsburgh: T. M. Walker, 1909), pp. 83-84.

CONTENTS

HARD TIMES COME AGAIN NO MORE

INTRODUCTION

Another Book on Suffering?

Faith is the bird that feels the light
And sings while the dawn is still darkness.
— RABINDRANATH TAGORE[1]

D o we really need another book on suffering? This subject, despite being a perennial theme in human history, has been tackled by a long and impressive list of capable writers, and some of them have works that might be considered definitive. But there is nothing definitive about our human attempts to come to grips with hard times. Each new generation and each new life joins the struggle afresh. So new windows on the great mystery always seem welcome.

This work is not the first or most comprehensive and certainly not the last word on suffering. It is born of my own struggles and of my dissatisfaction with the answers that come too easily to our lips when we are faced with hard times. Honesty demands that we approach suffering knowing that no rational word can make sense of the loss and the pain. I have often spoken through my own darkness, saying things I did not believe but hoped desperately to believe once more—that God was close and redemption was assured.

The episodes related in this book offer a kaleidoscopic vision of how people of faith might approach hard times—as an unwelcome visitor, a spur to wisdom, and an ultimately toothless villain. The first great American popular composer, Stephen Foster, provides the theme song for this journey. I discovered his tune "Hard Times Come Again No More" about ten years ago, and it has haunted me since. It haunts this book as well, as does the poignant story of Foster's life.

Another prominent figure in these pages is Job, the Bible's hardy handyman when it comes to suffering. It is a testament to the craft and power of the biblical story that Job still speaks to us today. The third major figure in this book is an unnamed foreign woman who comes to Jesus with a request for her daughter's healing and ends up fighting for a blessing. Her story joins those of contemporary people facing down their own hard times.

My thanks as always to those who accompany me on my journeys through wonder and worry: the people of Franktown Church, who have welcomed me into their lives and who grant me space for explorations like these; Suzanne, Joel, and Rachel, my beloved family members who see too little of me when the writing is going on and who have loved me through many a dark day; Bill Joyner, who inspired me to write in the first place; Lisa Stevens Powers, Hogan Pesaniello, Eugene Rogers, and many more. Deane Root and Kathryn Miller Haines gave me their time, wisdom, and assistance as I worked in the Stephen Foster Collection, University of Pittsburgh. Edward Ayers, who is still my favorite nineteenth-century historian even though he now moonlights as the president of the University of Richmond, helped with a well-timed conversation. Sarah Snyder transcribed long interviews. You were all grace and light to me in this project.

Finally, this book is dedicated to the memory of Barbara Tankard, whose own struggle with cancer and her joy and faith in facing it were a great inspiration to me as this book began to take form.

1. Spirit

(or Learning from Hard Times)

And my lament
Is cries countless, cries like dead letters sent
To dearest him that lives alas! away.
　　　　　　　—GERARD MANLEY HOPKINS[1]

In the dark years of the American Civil War, the most popular composer of the day was living in poverty and relative obscurity in New York City. By 1862 he was alone in spare quarters, separated from his wife, who had left with their daughter to try and make it on her own as a telegraph operator in New Jersey. Years removed from his latest hit song, he began to drink heavily and to fall into despair.

Even though his songs continued to sell well and were part of the general culture, Stephen Foster did not see much revenue from them. Poor deals with publishers meant that he received royalties far below what he should have gotten, and to make ends meet he sold off future rights to his songs. Had he been living in the contemporary era, he would have made millions from his music. As it was, he was reduced to begging help from his brother, Morrison, to pay for laundry bills.[2]

The words of songs such as "O Susannah," "Camptown Races," "My Old Kentucky Home," "Nelly Bly," and the wistful "Old Folks at Home" tripped easily from the lips of those he

17

passed in the streets. The words spoke to a generation that hoped that somewhere in this constantly moving American society, with all its change and upheaval, was a place to call home. One song in particular seemed to take on special meaning as the war dragged on and soldiers left to fight, some never returning home. Written almost a decade before the war, Foster's "Hard Times Come Again No More" found new life among soldier and civilian alike.

The song features a "pale, drooping maiden" weighed down by the evils that had come her way and that lingered "around my cabin door." With gentle defiance, the singer commands, "Hard Times, come again no more." By the fourth verse the command becomes a universal cry for every suffering person, wafting over the waves, heard upon the shore, and uttered at the side of the grave. The Civil War left many graves beside which mourners could sing about hard times.

While his songs and his name were well-known, Foster himself was not. He spent his days playing music in dingy bars. He was still writing songs, mostly in collaboration with George Cooper, another struggling musician. Cooper handled most of the lyrics, but both words and music fell far below the quality of Foster's early work. Some were simply drinking songs delighting in the momentary amnesia that drunkenness can bring:

> Darkling sorrows take their flight
> In the wine's rich ruby light,
> And the hours are winged with pleasures
> While the bowl goes round.[3]

There was even an ode to moustaches. Foster's mental state began to deteriorate to the point that he had trouble remembering the words to all his songs save one: "Hard Times."[4]

So it might seem unusual that in the midst of this period of wandering through a struggle with alcohol, Foster turned up one night at a temperance reception in the Bowery. John Mahon, an Irish journalist living in the city, befriended Foster and invited him to come to the gathering. During the night the group began to sing, and Mahon asked Foster to take a turn. Mahon tells the story as this broken man sang out the words to the one song he clung to:

> [H]e threw such pathos into his voice, especially when he came to the word: "There's a poor little maiden who weeps her life away," that there wasn't a dry eye in the room. Every voice was hushed. All crowded round him; and as he came to the chorus: "'Tis the song, 'tis the sigh of the weary / Hard times! hard times come again no more; / Many days you have lingered around my cabin-door — / Oh, hard times come again no more" there arose such a burst of melody from the untutored (musically, I mean) male and female voices present as I never heard before or since.

It was only after the singer sat down that the host finally introduced him as Stephen C. Foster, "the author and composer not only of that, but of some of the finest songs ever written." The gathering erupted in cheers with handkerchiefs waving in what Mahon referred to as a "perfect ovation." It was one of the few moments of public recognition for Foster and for the power of that song.[5]

It may seem strange to begin a book about suffering and hope with such a bittersweet tale. Perhaps it's even stranger because Stephen Foster was no paragon of virtue or pious model of noble suffering. He was just one more fellow wanderer who found his way into hard times through the usual combination of personal failings, social ills, sins of omission and commission, and what we sometimes call bad luck. For Foster there would be no happy ending. Before the war ended or his circumstances changed, he died following a fall in his small room.

What Foster left, however, was a song—testimony to an enduring spirit within humanity that refuses to let hard times have the last word over our lives. In its stark images and haunting melody, "Hard Times Come Again No More" lets us feel the reality of suffering in this world, the poignancy of loss, and the longing for a new day, and then it emits a cry that pushes back against the darkness. It is no anthem of faith. It is a window on the wounded soul. And because we all know that wound to some degree, the song has the capacity to move us, like that Bowery audience, to tears and to sing its chorus at full throat. From those gathered in a Civil War–era reception to modern recordings by the likes of Bob Dylan and Emmylou Harris, "Hard Times" endures as a heart cry.

The Value of Hard Times

Hard times used to be good for us. At least, that's how our popular culture often presented them. In the nineteenth century, Stephen Foster invited the comfortably placed audience that purchased his music to "pause in life's pleasures and count its many tears" because it was an edifying exercise. There was a certain nobility in struggle. Literature gives us many examples. Would we have seen Oliver Twist's character without the bleakness of the orphanage? Would Atticus Finch of *To Kill a Mockingbird* have stood so tall in the courtroom if he hadn't been a Depression-era widower with two small children? How could we know Celie from *The Color Purple* except through her empowering journey through racism and sexism?

When twenty-first-century Bruce Wayne (aka Batman) experiences hard times, it doesn't look the same. Wayne, one of the spate of superheroes flooding our movie screens these days, doesn't have to struggle with economic deprivation. He broods over what to do with his powers from the comfort of a mansion while advised by his wise butler. It is not what he lacks that defines him but what he is going to do with his abundance.

Maybe it's time to listen to "Hard Times" again. When the stock market tanked in the fall of 2008, it seemed to usher in a new post-abundance era. Lingering wars in Iraq and Afghanistan showed us the limits of military might to bring anything resembling peace. The ongoing horrors of genocidal conflicts in central Africa reveal the persistence of sexual violence and other acts of inhumanity. When we look into our own hearts, we know the dark shadows and the old wounds. We don't have to look far for hard times.

It is a peculiar term: *hard times*. It has a particular connection to economic struggles, and Stephen Foster wrote his song in 1854 during an economic downturn. But the term and the song were evocative enough that they lived on in very different kinds of hard times.

We think we would like to live in a world without hard times, but the truth is that pain can give us important information. Gabby Gingras is a young Minnesota child who doesn't feel pain. When she gets a shot at the doctor, she doesn't wince. When it's cold outside, she doesn't feel it. These may not seem like problems, but without the sensation of pain Gabby also faces life-threatening situations. When she is injured, she may not know it. When she began cutting teeth, she would mash down on her gums until she bled. As a result she had to have all her teeth pulled. She began to scratch her eyes without knowing that she was doing damage. Her left eye has been removed because of the injury.

Trish Gingras, Gabby's mother, says their family has learned that pain is an essential tutor: "Pain teaches. Pain protects. Pain can save you from a lot of bad things in life."[6] Without pain, Trish's daughter has to spend her life under constant supervision, wearing goggles and other protective gear.

So what do we learn from the hard times of life? What will we learn by spending time in their company? Let's start by going to the ash heap.

The View from the Ash Heap

The biblical treatment of hard times gets its most extensive expression in the book of Job. It is an ancient story (actually, in its present form it may be two or more stories pulled together), and it steadfastly refuses to let easy answers to suffering suffice. There is a happy ending, but it is not particularly satisfying, and questions hover around the characters—including the character of God.

The opening scene threatens to turn Job into a mere pawn in some heavenly game. God makes a wager with the Satan, who is not the red devil with pointed tail that we sometimes imagine when we use that term, but rather the appointed investigator for the courts of heaven. The Satan wanders to and fro through the land seeking out the true hearts of humanity. In Job he finds a man he really wants to test.

God likes Job. God holds him up as a model of faithfulness and integrity. The Satan is unimpressed. He wonders what would happen if Job were not so blessed with children, cattle, and riches. So God strikes up a bargain and allows the Satan to wreak havoc on Job. Job's children die, his cattle and property are struck down, and his wealth is wiped out in an instant. In a second round of calamities, Job's very body is afflicted, and he breaks out in sores from his head to his feet. He goes to sit among the ashes of his former life and scrapes his lesions with the shard of a broken pot.

Job's wife comes to him and offers cold comfort: "Are you still hanging on to your integrity? Why don't you just curse God and die?"

To which Job replies, "Don't be foolish. Should we accept the good things from God and not accept the evil?"

The Bible says Job didn't sin during any of this, but that last question really sticks. When God sends us evil, how should we react? Does God send us evil? This line of inquiry dominates the rest of the book of Job. Job's friends come to be with him in his desolation, and for about a week they get it right. They simply sit there with him in silence. But then they start talking, and what they discuss is the question that haunted Stephen Foster and minds great and small from time immemorial: Why do hard times come, and how should we respond?

A Fate Worse than Fate

If the Job story ended there, that question might have a very disturbing answer: hard times come because there is something working actively *against* us. It is worse than fate or chance.

If bad things happen just because the universe is made in such a way that bad things are an inevitable part of life, that is scary but understandable. The world runs according to some grand physical laws that ensure that the system as a whole survives, but along the way individuals sometimes suffer loss and ruin, and all of us eventually suffer death. You can't complain about the moral injustice of a world created like this. You can't cry out against the death of an infant or the flooding of a nor'easter because those are just part of the grand scheme of things. If we did not believe in a God who cares for and is intimately involved in the universe, we would not have any reason to ask why hard times come. Hard times come because they are the way of the world.

Fate, too, is a little easier to swallow. Fate says that what occurs is in some sense foreordained. Hard times happen because they were determined beforehand, and the proper response to them is to accept your fate grimly and perhaps with some dignity. But fate places God far in the background; in fact, fate is itself a kind of god—an uncaring, unconcerned force that we can condemn with loud, righteous anger, but to what effect? No one ever said that fate cared about us.

Christians, however, do say that God cares about us, and so the question of suffering is one with which people who believe in a loving God must seriously struggle. We have no grounds to question the injustice of suffering if there is no such God, because without that God there is no moral agent at the center of the universe. If we did not believe, when we cry to the heavens, to whom would we call out?

Some may chide believers for their naïveté in holding on to a world where God still lives, but what would we be left with if we did *not* hold on, except a disenchanted world that offers no ultimate reconciliation, no comfort, and no redemption for the sufferer? Believers must struggle with a universe where suffering matters and where hard times point to the deepest questions of life and death.

The book of Job offers a chilling introduction to that struggle. It suggests that the world is not just a neutral sphere in which good and bad things happen and there is some kind of cosmic equilibrium to the whole thing. In Job's world there are agents afoot, wandering the earth here and yon, walking to and fro, seeking to do us ill. We could end up as the Satan's playthings.

God has intentions for us, just as God had intentions for Job. The story tells us that God seeks human beings who will be perfectly upright, fearing God and turning away from evil. But even those who live God-fearing, evil-despising lives are not immune from the forces that work against God's intentions. We will be battered, but the question is whether we can see, in the shadows and deaths of this life, the world God is bringing to birth.

Fingernail Faith

I admit that I am a fingernail Christian. There are times when I feel that I am holding on to my faith by my fingernails. I am ever grateful that my relationship with God is not determined by how well I am able to hold onto my theology on a given day, because there are many days when it is shaken.

We could pick up the newspaper on any day and find something that would shake us to our core. In early 2010 it was an earthquake that devastated Haiti. In 2006 it was a story in Pennsylvania. In October of that year, Charles Carl Roberts, plagued by who-knows-what demons, went into an Amish schoolhouse, sent out the adults and the boys, and then shot the ten girls. It was an unspeakable act. It is the kind of thing that makes you reach for your children and pull them close.

It is also the kind of thing that, had it happened in another community with other people, might have played out very much like other American tragedies. There would have been televised funeral services with speakers from across the country. There would have been chain-link fences covered in ribbons, and teddy bears, and reporters trying to wrench every bit of anguish they could from the traumatized survivors.

That sort of spectacle was on the sidelines in this case, though, because the Amish are a different sort of community. Deeply religious, they have their own ways. The world watched from a distance as they began the burials. Thirty-four horse-drawn buggies made their way through the farmland for the first of the funerals. The funerals were held in homes, according to Amish tradition.

Two ministers presided, and one of them told the story of the earth's creation from the book of Genesis. Not much was said about the deceased, because the focus was on God—how God's love filled the whole world, how God's love created this beautiful yet tragically scarred earth and all its peoples, how God will continue to do the work of creation until all the work is done and all the children are brought home. The Amish community buried little Naomi Rose Ebersol, seven years old, in a plain, handmade white dress and a very simple coffin. Then they went to funerals for Marian and Mary Liz and Lena. The next day they buried Anna Mae.[7] Hard times? They don't come any harder.

In the midst of their grief, these people did something else that did not fit the usual pattern. As families made food for those who grieved, they took some to Marie Roberts, the wife of the man who had killed the children before killing himself. They took her food because they knew she had suffered a loss too. They invited her to attend one of the funerals. They offered their forgiveness, because that is what Christians are told to do—told to do because it does not come naturally. What comes naturally is to hate and to strike out and to flail against a world in which such funerals have to take place. But even in such darkness, when the forces of death threaten to overcome us, God is willing life, and we know that because these Amish people, whose lives were formed by a savior who submitted even to death on a cross, brought food and forgiveness instead of bitterness and more darkness.

Theologian David Bentley Hart writes that the Christian vision of the world is not an easy one. It is, he says, a "moral and spiritual labor. The Christian eye sees (or should see) a deeper truth in the world than mere 'nature,' and it is a truth that gives rise not to optimism but to joy."[8] In the valley of the shadow of death, it is not easy to see joy. In hard times, we are right to believe that things are not as they should be and that evil is not what God intends. Indeed, there are forces afoot in the universe that would resist God's will even though they cannot have ultimate victory. But we should not cover over the moral and spiritual labor of our struggle with suffering by saying that God somehow gives us evil so as to bring about a greater good. Evil is never the will of God. God does not need the death of a child in order to be great.

The Grounding Conviction

God is making all things new and will not lose anything or any-one in bringing this to be—at least, that is the conviction moti-vating this book. I know how easy it is to turn on God. All it took was five minutes in the car, driving away from the hospital as my grandmother lay incapacitated from a stroke, for me to begin shouting out loud to You Know Who, "Don't you dare! Don't you dare touch her. Don't you dare bring her pain. Don't you dare take her from me." As if God would author such an end for such a woman. As if God were not in the love I felt as I held her hand, even in such a state. As if God had suddenly become an alien force.

I approach this book as one who needs to hear that God's grace is more than just a piety easily mouthed until hard times show up at the door. Perhaps you are someone who needs to hear that too. Sometimes I catch the most powerful glimpses of God's presence from the periphery, as it were—in the roughness of lives like Stephen Foster's and in the beauty of art like his that captures something essential about who we are. Perhaps you are someone who catches those glimpses too.

Hard times threaten darkness, but they may also illuminate an underlying richness and texture that pervade this world. As for-getful people who easily turn on God and then just as easily forget who they are and how wonderfully and fearfully they were made, perhaps we need a raw, bracing wind to blow every now and then to save us from the illusions we so desperately cling to. If nothing else, hard times may help us pay attention.

2. Longing

(or A Thousand Miles from Home)

Weep no more, my lady,
Oh! weep no more today!
We will sing one song
For the old Kentucky Home,
For the old Kentucky Home, far away . . .

A few more days for to tote the weary load,
No matter, 'twill never be light;
A few more days till we totter on the road,
Then my old Kentucky Home, good-night!
—STEPHEN FOSTER[1]

The Pale, Drooping Maiden

When Stephen Foster sat down in 1854 to write the words to a new tune he had been working on, the first phrase he marked in his sketchbook was "There's a pale drooping maiden."[2] It was an image that persisted with him. Six years later he published another song, "Poor Drooping Maiden," about a young woman

Slavery and Minstrel Music

It was a nostalgia shared by many of his compatriots. When Foster wrote songs about people far from home, it resonated with a population that was being uprooted by the changes in American society. Sometimes Foster used the figure of Southern slaves to express this longing. Though he never lived in the South and had little direct experience of slavery, he imagined a connection with slaves who lived with the threat of being separated from their families and who had close experience with hard labor and sorrow.

As he wrote "Hard Times," the bestselling book of the day was Harriet Beecher Stowe's *Uncle Tom's Cabin*—a seminal novel of the abolition movement, which gave a human face to slavery. What the book did was to put "the image of the broken black family at the center of American popular culture," according to historian Edward Ayers. "The reason that *Uncle Tom's Cabin* was so powerful is precisely because it translated the travails of black people into the domestic ideal—the mother-centered ideal, the Christian ideal that would have been the primary way that white, middle-class readership would have understood the social life of the greatest good. And so, it's not an accident that the most enduring image from . . . *Uncle Tom's Cabin* is the woman escaping across the ice with a baby in her arms."[8]

In his songs, Foster had already been tapping into an image of the domestic struggles of slaves. He wrote much of his early music in the form expected by the popular minstrel shows of his day—with exaggerated black dialect that sounds offensive to modern ears—but the perspective of his lyrics reveals nobility in the slave. The individual caught in slavery is a preeminent example, for Foster, of the experience of every person who feels the pain of separation and the trials of this life. So the singer of another of Foster's well-known songs, "Old Folks at Home," can

32

say: "All the world is sad and dreary, everywhere I roam . . . far from the old folks at home."[9]

A More Formal Language of the Spirit

When Foster left behind the rough-hewn songs of the blackface minstrel shows, he began using new language to speak to a different audience—one that expected a more cultured perspective. Foster knew this world. He was immersed in the Romantic poetry of his day and was able to read and translate from French and German. He knew what that audience expected, and it wasn't a world of banjos and horse races. They wanted a more formal language of the spirit.

When I read Foster's lyrics, I am struck by how distant his characters seem to be. Even when he is describing deep, passionate feelings, there is a sense of separation. His singer dreams of Jeanie with the light brown hair (often thought to be a reference to his wife, Jane) but knows that she has "vanished and her sweet songs flown." In another song, the singer longs for a day when he can "roam the plain / Joyous and free" with the inaccessible Laura Lee.[10] In "Hard Times," the travails of the "frail forms" are outside the door, in sharp contrast to the interior, where "we seek mirth and beauty and music light and gay." The singer observes the "pleading looks" of the unfortunate sufferers, but there is no interaction with them.

"There is this distance . . . this yearning, longing, [and] unapproachability" in the poetry of the day, according to Deane Root. "You can't approach, you can never touch."[11] The term often used to describe this distance is the German word *Sehnsucht*—something that defies easy translation. It is a compound of the verb "to long for" and the noun "addiction."[12] This longing has the character of a kind of homesickness that leaves us permanently unsettled.

voice would be merry," the maiden is instead sighing in despair because Hard Times have come to her.

Foster's Own Hard Times

Hard times must have seemed a constant enemy to Stephen Foster too. He was prone to melancholy. A later acquaintance would note that "weeping came to him far more easily than smiling,"[14] and the events of this period in his life were only deepening his struggles.

He married his wife, Jane, in 1850, and their relationship was troubled. Jane had difficulty adapting to Foster's career, which he was inventing as he went along. No one had ever been a professional songwriter before, and Foster was trying to make it work with no guides. But his dedication to the task and his need for silence mystified Jane. "They were incompatible spiritually in some way because she was not musical," says Root. "She could not understand his passion, his devotion, and this was his life."[15]

Stephen and Jane had a daughter, Marion, in 1851, but they would never be settled. The couple separated in 1853, and Foster determined to pursue his craft in New York City. A year later the family reunited and lived in Hoboken, New Jersey, for a time. Then, with his parents ailing back home near Pittsburgh, Foster left again to be with them. Jane and Marion apparently followed a few weeks later. This was the period during which Foster was writing "Hard Times."

His parents would both die within the year. "Hard Times" was published early in 1855 and was a modest success. Even so, Foster's career and financial situation were beginning to decline. In 1857 he sold the rights to many of his most popular songs to his music publisher, Firth, Pond and Co. Later, deeply in debt to the publisher, he would sell even more.[16] Soldiers in the armies fighting the Civil War were singing clever parodies of "Hard Times" to lament their often stale bread provisions ("Hard tack come again no more"), but the composer of the song was struggling to survive.

By July of 1861, the Fosters had separated again. Stephen kept a residence in New York while Jane took a job as a railroad telegraph operator in Pennsylvania.[17] Foster's decline deepened. He began a partnership with George Cooper, a lyricist who collaborated with him on a number of forgettable songs. Much of what they made from the songs went back into alcohol.

John Mahon, the Irish journalist who befriended Foster during the time, remembered his first encounter with him: "I was standing in Windust's restaurant in Park Row, one day, with one or two other journalists, when my attention was attracted by a short man . . . who was very neatly dressed in a blue swallow-tailed coat, high silk hat, and-so-forth (the and-so-forth I forget). This gentleman walked up to the bar, took his drink, and was turning away, when Mr. E. D. Barry, the barkeeper, whispered to me: 'That is Stephen C. Foster, the great song-writer!' "[18]

The contrast between the legendary composer and the actual man only grew. Another visitor, encountering him in a bar room a year later, was struck by his well-worn clothes and "soft brown eyes, somewhat dimmed by dissipation. . . . It was hard for me to force myself to believe that poor, wretched-looking object was at that moment the most popular song-composer in the world; but it was Foster himself!"[19] Foster seemed to be receding. The same observer noted, "He would walk, talk, eat and drink with you, and yet always seem distant, maintaining an awkward dignity, if I may so term it. Whether it was a natural bashfulness, or a voluntary reserve, I can not say, but those who know him most intimately were never familiar."[20]

The longing for a home remained. One of his songs from the period, "A Thousand Miles from Home," expresses the desire:

Far from my childhood's scenes, with weary steps I roam;
Laden with weight of care, a thousand miles from home

. . . .

Oh! how the heart will droop a thousand miles from home.[21]

What home, if any, Foster might have imagined as he penned these words was more than just a location. There was no place a thousand miles or further where he could feel this sense of belonging.

As other songs faded from his memory, the words of "Hard Times" remained, and in the repeated chorus there is a refuge—a cabin, within which the likes of the pale, drooping maiden could resist, however weakly, the hard times at the door. One of the last songs to bear Foster's name turns that image to express contentment. Dated 1864, the year of his death, the song "Sitting by My Own Cabin Door" affirms that

The waves of trouble on the sea,
The whirlwinds on the moor,
Can bring no sorrow now to me,
For I'm sitting by my own cabin door.[22]

Searching for Faith

Foster was the sort of person you worry over. Like many an artist of his era, he seems to have suffered more tragedy than he should have. We wish for him an agent, a therapist, a soul friend, and a faith that could steer him through the challenges he faced. Perhaps then he would not have known such misery and hardship.

The few surviving letters from his family members indicate that they had these same concerns for him. In a letter to his brother Morrison in 1859, Foster's sister Henrietta chides the two brothers for their neglect of the church. "I beg of you . . . to hearken to [Jesus'] voice, when he calls you to give him your heart. Give up all the vain and unsatisfying things of life, and dedicate your self, your soul, and body, to his service. . . . How often would I have put my arms around your neck and implored you to think of these things, and not only think, but act."[23]

The words reflect a sincere Victorian piety, but there is no evidence that Foster responded. He would probably have confessed an allegiance to Christian faith if asked. Morrison Foster, in remembering his brother years later, would say that he "was a firm belivere (sic) in the gospel of Christ. & ever had an abiding confidence in his mercy."[24]

That is about the extent of the known faith of Stephen Foster. But another sort of faith is latent in his music. It is transmitted through the language of desire, of imagining a place and time where true love can be realized and where struggles are ended. For Foster, this is often located in an inaccessible past or in a place where it is impossible to go. Death, distance, and of course hard times are barriers that thwart our longings. But there is nobility in what remains. There is a piercing quality to the cry the singer lifts. It says, "Despite the weariness, the song, the sigh of the weary goes on."

The Language of Desire

The language of desire is not foreign to Christian faith. The popular twentieth-century writer C. S. Lewis was something of an apostle of *Sehnsucht*, relating that yearning to the longing for a lasting home. Lewis reflects an ancient theme in Christian writing that finds its classic expression in Augustine's *Confessions*: "Our hearts are restless till they rest in Thee."[25] Whereas Foster often expresses that longing in nostalgia for something lost, Lewis concentrates on glimpses of joy and looks ahead in hope. Writing to Dom Bede Griffiths in 1959, Lewis notes:

> It is just when there seems to be most of Heaven already here that I come nearest to longing for a patria. It is the bright frontispiece which whets one to read the story itself. All joy (as distinct from mere pleasure, still more amusement) emphasizes our pilgrim status; always reminds, beckons, awakens desire. Our best havings are wantings.[26]

Lewis was capable of looking deeply into the tragic dimensions of life, as well. Two of his most affecting books are *The Problem of Pain* and *A Grief Remembered*. But he was interested in pain and grief perhaps for the same reason that Foster began "Hard Times" with the strange invitation to "pause in life's pleasures and count its many tears": the essence of the human animal is on glancing display when hard times assail. And when stripped of all else, "what we are" is revealed as a yearning. In the brokenness of time, we yearn for something that is more solid, more complete, more lasting than what we know. Suffering unveils a holy discontent within us that seeks a hearing and a healing, and ultimately a home.

What Lewis adds to this deep awareness of brokenness is the confidence that the restlessness is more than the engine driving us; it is also guiding us to healing. In *The Problem of Pain* he writes:

> All the things that have ever deeply possessed your soul have been but hints of [the thing you were born desiring]—tantalizing glimpses, promises never quite fulfilled, echoes that died away just as they caught your ear. But if it should really become manifest—if there ever came an echo that did not die away but swelled into the sound itself—you would know it. Beyond all possibility of doubt you would say, "Here at last is the thing I was made for." We cannot tell each other about it. It is the secret signature of each soul, the incommunicable and unappeasable want, the thing we desired before we met our wives or made our friends or chose our work, and which we shall still desire on our deathbeds, when the mind no longer knows wife or friend or work. While we are, this is. If we lose this, we lose all.[27]

The strains of "Hard Times" make a poignant accompaniment to the human journey. Stephen Foster's heartbreak produced a work of art that could bear the burdens of many other yearning souls and give voice to future generations facing very different kinds of hard times. The song endures because it touches something basic about our human experience and lifts it up so that it cannot be ignored.

3. Anger

(or "I Will Not Be Extinguished")

God has made my heart faint;
Shaddai has terrified me.
But I will not be extinguished in the face of darkness,
when my face is covered by thick darkness.
— Job 23:16-17[1]

Anger in the Ashes

When we last saw Job, he was sitting on an ash heap. His world had come crashing down around him, the result of forces that he could not control and that were actively working against him. When a series of unfortunate events happen to a person, we sometimes say that God or the devil had it in for that one. When we say that, we probably don't mean it. It's just a dramatic way of saying, "Wow! You really are bad off." But it really was true for Job. Somebody *did* have it in for him. The Satan was the agent, but God was the accomplice. It may just be a fanciful story told as a test case for the persistence of faith in the face of suffering, but when we stop to consider Job's condition, whether he's fictional or real, we can't help but be overwhelmed by what happened to him. Here is a good man—a perfectly upright man!—who suffers unjustly. We are supposed to be scandalized by that.

43

it. I can lay out the case. I can make the argument. I can take whatever explanation you throw at me, because I'm convinced you will agree with me. Even you will admit that what has happened to me is unjust. Even you, holy and terrible as your name is, must take my side. So now all I have to do is find you. I'm weary. I'm terrified because of what has happened to me. But I will not be extinguished in the face of the darkness."

There's a lot of dispute about that last verse. The text is so old and corrupted that it is hard to make out what the Hebrew means. Some translations have Job saying, "If only I could vanish in the darkness."[3] But it seems to me that the tone of Job's speech here is one of defiance. He is not trying to vanish. He is anguished because it seems that *God* has vanished, and Job wants to make his case. Job will not "go gentle into that good night," to borrow a phrase from Dylan Thomas.[4]

So, if we are looking to this story for a model in dealing with hard times, then there is a lot more here than the patience of Job. Part of Job's integrity comes from his belief in a universe where there is justice at work, where there is a moral center and God is in control. Job trusts that, if he can gain a hearing with God, God will side with him. The darkness will not reduce him to silence.

Making Sense of the Senseless

One of the challenges of a pastor's life is that you are often called upon to go into situations where some senseless thing has taken place and try to make some sense of it all. Such a time came to me on a beautiful Saturday afternoon in a central Virginia spring. I was sitting on the porch of the old farmhouse-style parsonage that was our home. So many things seemed to be flourishing. Fertility was in the air. I was preparing for a move to the university as a student and campus pastor. Our house was alive with the sounds and activity of our two young children. The sunset that day behind the distant Blue Ridge Mountains was beautiful.

Just a few miles away, a young man got into his car to go to his senior prom. He was driving into the sun, going a little too fast, and as he made a turn on a small country road he lost control of the vehicle. He died at the scene. That's when the local responders called me.

His parents were away in another state, and I was asked to make the call to them. "There has been an accident," I heard myself say. Those five words brought to life the fear that parents carry with them when they are separated from their children. What did I go on to say? I don't remember. But I did learn that the victim's younger brother was home by himself.

I found the boy, of middle-school age, alone in the dark and silence. The living room was bare, the only light in the room an old table lamp sitting on the floor. We sat together on a worn couch and waited for his parents. I felt a destitution of words. So we sat. And the world was not right.

A month later, there was another accident involving another teenager, this one a young woman who had been adopted by the whole community. Diagnosed with a kidney ailment as a baby, she had spent most of her life on dialysis. We had celebrated with her when she had become a teenager and, receiving a kidney transplant from her mother, had discovered that she could live a more normal life. She was just starting to enjoy what this new gift would mean for her. Then there was the accident.

At the service, the funeral home was packed. Cars were lined up for over a half-mile. All her friends were there. All the community was there. Her grieving mother was on the front row. And what could I say to this group? That God's purpose for the world included this girl's death? That committing some dire sin in her life made her deserving of this end? No. I did not believe that. Job would not have believed that either.

What I offered that day was an angry sermon, because I felt that anger was the most faithful thing any of us had to offer. It was not that God could not redeem even that situation, because God does overcome even death; there is an empty tomb that proclaims it. But someone had to say, "No more. One day there will be no more funerals like this. One day we will see all the tombs emptied and all the forces defeated that would bring death upon us."

Covering Over the Madness

When we affirm that bad things are part of God's purpose, even when we make such claims innocently and sincerely, we are trying to cover over the madness. When hard times come, they always seem senseless and threaten to make a mockery of our beliefs. When we try to establish a reason for tsunamis or murders or illnesses such as AIDS, we are desperately seeking assurance that, even though the world seems unhinged, someone somewhere is still in control.

The evil thing about evil is that it *doesn't* make sense, can't make sense, refuses to make sense. Our response to it should not be to domesticate it but to spit in its face, to defy its pretense to ultimate power, to laugh at its absurdity, and to recognize the stakes because they are high. If God is not the opponent and vanquisher of evil, then the universe as the realm of God's glory and reconciliation falls apart. If God does not reject evil, then there is no point to the struggle. If God is not unalterably set against hard times, then what is Jesus doing in this world?

Yes, what about Jesus? If Job is a model, what more do we learn from Christ? The theologian David Bentley Hart says that "if it is from Christ that we are to learn how God relates himself to sin, suffering, evil, and death, it would seem that he provides us little evidence of anything other than a regal, relentless, and miraculous enmity: sin he forgives, suffering he heals, evil he casts out, and death he conquers. And absolutely nowhere does Christ act as if any of these things are part of the eternal work or purposes of God."[5]

But doesn't this make God less powerful than we want to believe? If God is strong enough to bring the universe into being and loving enough to claim us as children of God, what explains the persistence of bad things happening to good and bad people? Don't we have to believe, for the sake of God's love and power, that all this evil must be serving a greater good?

All things ultimately will serve this God. God is reconciling all things in Christ Jesus. But God's reconciling work takes place in a broken world fragmented in so many ways and operating in ruptured time.

For Christians, the course of history is clear. In the end, love does win the day. The tomb is empty, and all the wounded are made whole. Our calling is to see the world as God sees it at the end of all things. God is making all things new, even in the darkness, and we shall not be extinguished by the dark.

The Cry That Disrupts the World

One way of looking at the problem of suffering is through the long lens that sees every human moment as just a small piece of a much larger mosaic. It is the sort of sky view that leads people to downplay the importance of individual instances when hard times come. What's the point of complaining if we're part of a bigger, more comprehensive picture? Will this suffering matter in fifty years? A hundred? If it all gets redeemed at the end of time and heaven is there as a solace, then does this moment really have much significance?

The stories of individuals who exhibit life in the midst of suffering inspire me to think that these questions are entirely misplaced and are expressed exactly the wrong way around. The better question is: If there is beauty and order and some ungraspable sense in the larger picture of the universe, then every moment is filled with a notion of the eternal. It is in the small pieces of the broken mirror of time that we get a reflection, however partial, of a reality more real than what we have been living.

In his book *The End of Suffering: Finding Purpose in Pain*, the poet Scott Cairns points out the clarifying effects of affliction. "Under most circumstances," he says, "the occasions of our suffering are capable of revealing what our habitual illusions often obscure, keeping us from knowing. Our afflictions drag us—more or less kicking—into a fresh and vivid awareness that we are not in control of our circumstances, that we are not quite whole, that our days are salted with affliction."[6] If we deny these truths when experiencing good times—our lack of control, our brokenness, our close association with hard times—then suffering can help us see more clearly the heart of this human reality.

This makes the individual human experience of suffering supremely important. Even Josef Stalin was onto the truth of this with the perverse aphorism often credited to him (perhaps erroneously): "One death is a tragedy; one million is a statistic."[7] Hard times win when the sufferer disappears behind a veil that can be labeled genocide or Holocaust or earthquake. But when there is a poor, drooping maiden to stand before us—or a defiant man on an ash heap, or an inexplicably joyful woman with a chemo pump—then evil is no longer allowed to carry the narrative. The main character demands to be seen in all of her particularity.

This is one of the great insights of liberation theologies, particularly in their Latin American expressions. When people become objects, submerged beneath historical forces and ideologies, they lose their particularity. Suffering imposes a blanket of silence on people, forbidding them from being seen as anything other than a victim.

Job seeks to throw off the blanket of silence. He will not let go of the fundamental contradiction between the faith of his friends and his own experience of God's justice. Job feels that if he does not speak up, in effect he will be accepting suffering (and the blame for it). He speaks up to maintain his integrity and to preserve his sense of meaning and purpose for the cosmos. Even when all the meaning-making structures in his life have failed him, Job does not lose his confidence that beyond the darkness there is a force pulling the world together. And while he waits for that force to be revealed, he will not be appeased and he will not be extinguished.

For this, his friends accuse him of arrogance. Arrogance and disturbing the peace have always been the charges thrown at those who argue for justice. Like the clergymen Martin Luther King, Jr., addressed in his "Letter from the Birmingham Jail," those who are disturbed by the cry of the suffering argue that if the oppressed would just accept their lot, in time it will all make sense. Who are the sufferers to try and set the world right? Who are they to speak for God? But Job knows that the only way he can honor the fire within him is to lift it to the heavens and trust that an answer will come.

Anger and Irony

We live in an age in which Job-like defiance is looked upon with suspicion. Anger, we feel, is the stock-in-trade of the wingnuts—the fringe elements of our political life, left and right, whose earnestness and clarity are frightening to those of us who feel we are not so naïve about things. Like Job's friends, we would like to sit these people down and explain how things really work.

If anger is their thing, then ours often is irony. According to essayist Jedediah Purdy, "the point of irony is a quiet refusal to believe in the depth of relationships, the sincerity of motivation, or the truth of speech—especially earnest speech. In place of the romantic idea that each of us harbors a true self struggling for expression, the ironist offers the suspicion that we are all just quantum selves—all spin all the way down."[8] For Purdy, the embodiment of irony is Jerry Seinfeld, whose 1990s self-titled TV sitcom was populated by characters who seemed to have no core values of their own and who mocked the pretensions of those claiming strong convictions.

Irony protects us from passions that would unsettle us, and so we become commentators on the world rather than participants in it. We are painfully aware of how easily our tentative beliefs can be exposed. If we were to stake our lives on a truth or commit ourselves fully to a belief, surely we would be setting ourselves up for a fall when everything goes wrong.

When things do go wrong, though, irony is cold comfort. Derived from a Greek word meaning "dissembler," irony ultimately has nothing to offer but avoidance of truth or the dark notion that there is no truth. Job is not an ironist. He may bemoan his birth, but in his trials he is still a fiery believer. The ground on which his conviction is built may be uncertain in the midst of his devastation, but there is ground.

Over the long term, anger is not a desirable companion. Its

adrenaline turns bitter, and it clouds our vision. But anger may be a midwife to new days of light. It is a hedge against despair and a fierce guardian of dignity. And it can lead us to confront hard times with a faithfulness that reflects our deepest hopes and beliefs—hopes and beliefs that come from being formed by God and God's intentions for the world. In that way, even in darkness and defiance Job is an unlikely witness for the presence of God's goodness in the world. Which brings us to the story of another such witness.

4. Audacity

(or The Woman Who Wouldn't Go Away)

Jesus left that place and went away to the district of Tyre and Sidon. Just then a Canaanite woman from that region came out and started shouting, "Have mercy on me, Lord, Son of David; my daughter is tormented by a demon." But he did not answer her at all.

And his disciples came and urged him, saying, "Send her away, for she keeps shouting after us."

He answered, "I was sent only to the lost sheep of the house of Israel."

But she came and knelt before him, saying, "Lord, help me."

He answered, "It is not fair to take the children's food and throw it to the dogs."

She said, "Yes, Lord, yet even the dogs eat the crumbs that fall from their masters' table."

Then Jesus answered her, "Woman, great is your faith! Let it be done for you as you wish." And her daughter was healed instantly.

—MATTHEW 15:21-28

If there is a New Testament counterpart to Job, it may be the woman who confronts Jesus on his rare journey into the Gentile world. Whether she is called the Canaanite woman in Matthew's Gospel (15:21-31) or the Syrophoenician woman in Mark's (7:24-31), she, like Job, will not be extinguished. She stands out in contrast to other people who seek Jesus for healing, both

55

because she is initially denied it and because she will not accept no for an answer. In confronting Jesus, she too seems to call the God of Israel forth into the larger world to be its redeemer.

Just who does she think she is, this woman? According to the rules of the day, she had no right to do what she did. Jesus may have wandered into her territory, a Jewish teacher in a Gentile land, but that did not give her license to seek him out. To talk to him. To talk *theology* with him. Her gender, nationality, and religion would all have erected barriers.

Matthew's Gospel, in particular, emphasizes the Jewish character of Jesus' mission. Matthew sprinkles his narrative liberally with references to Jewish prophecies being fulfilled in Jesus. He attends synagogue, quotes Scripture, and observes Jewish religious holidays. So when this woman comes to him, it probably is no surprise that he outlines his mission as being "only to the lost sheep of the house of Israel."

However, this woman is like other audacious women Jesus meets in his journeys. There is the Samaritan woman at the well, another foreigner who ends up talking theology with him.[1] There is the woman with an unstaunched flow of blood, ritually unclean, who dares to touch him as he walks through a crowd.[2] There is the woman who breaks into a room where Jesus is sitting at table and anoints his feet with her tears, drying them with her hair.[3] All these women cross boundaries to find some form of healing.

Calling Out Jesus

When Jesus comes to her town, the Canaanite woman goes to him because she is driven by the one reality that defines her life—not her status or standing but the suffering of her daughter. That is the unavoidable fact of her existence. She goes to Jesus and begs him, "Have mercy on me, Lord, Son of David; my daughter is tormented by a demon." Is that a bit of flattery, recognizing Jesus by a Jewish messianic title? If it is intended that way, the sweet talk doesn't work. Jesus ignores her.

Wait a minute. Jesus ignores her? When did this Jesus show up? Our Sunday school image of Jesus "the meek and mild" has compassion for all and turns none away. After all, this is the Jesus who said, "Let the children come to me." Would he really condone the disciples barring this woman from his presence? But that is just what he does, reminding the disciples, presumably as the woman listens in, that his mission is to Israel.

It remains to the woman to call him out. She will not be talked *about* but insists on being talked *to*. If this man with a mission to Israel has left Israel, then maybe his actions suggest something more than his words say. If he is just being coy, testing her to see if she will accept his rejection, she is willing to play along. So she kneels before him. ("Worships him" might be a good translation from the original Greek. It's the same word used to describe the actions of three foreign visitors bearing gifts when they came before the infant Jesus. Even from the beginning, the world suspected that if Jesus had ultimate meaning for Israel, he must also have something to say to the nations.)

Kneeling, the woman cries, "Lord, help me!" The honorifics are gone. It is naked need that confronts Jesus now. Surely he won't turn away. Jesus responds, "It is not good to take the children's food and give it to the dogs."

Is Jesus really that ethnocentric? The people of Israel are children, and those who lie beyond are dogs—an ugly epithet in any day, but especially in Jesus' time?

Where does this Jesus come from? Is this an echo of the sarcastic God who shows up at the end of the book of Job, challenging the poor man to put his suffering into global perspective? Doesn't God value the concerns of one small person—or, in the case of the Canaanite woman, one small person outside the covenant community?

The woman does not back down. "Yes, Lord, but even the dogs eat the crumbs that fall from their master's table." The woman's faithful witness pulls this story back from the brink of an ugly ending. Despite her daughter's suffering and the woman's own rejection, she knows there is a circle of grace large enough to include her. Behind the world of walls and traditions that make this encounter between Jesus and the woman so difficult, there is a world where God is prodigally present, even in suffering. As the poet Gerard Manley Hopkins observed, "For all this, nature is never spent; / There lives the dearest freshness deep down things."[4]

We see faithful witness in Job's story as well, acknowledged in God's final address to Job. Though God puts Job in his place, we also see divine compassion and concern at work. In fact, God delights even in the details of a mountain goat's birth and the calving of a deer.[5] God sees and knows, and that knowing is universal.

This is the God to whom the Canaanite woman bears faithful witness. Jesus sees it, and his response is to praise her faith and to grant her request. However Jesus presented himself in their initial encounter, in responding to her challenge he reveals himself as the one who sees faithfulness even in those beyond the bounds of Israel. This woman has called out the Jesus who is hope for the whole world.

"You'll Be Free or Die"

We have traveled quite a distance from the "pale drooping maiden who toils her life away," the haunting figure in Stephen Foster's "Hard Times." In the Canaanite woman we encounter a more combative spirit, an heir to Job's fire, who is not content

58

with a world where demons can torment and God will be silent. Some time in her life, this woman has been schooled in justice, and she will speak out.

The abolitionist Harriet Tubman inherited some of that same fire. Born a slave on the Eastern Shore of Maryland, Tubman eventually escaped to freedom in the North, but she was not content while others remained enslaved. In the 1850s, while Foster was writing "Hard Times," Tubman was helping slaves escape them. At least nineteen times she returned to the South to help slaves move up the Underground Railroad to freedom. She carried a gun and used it to threaten the fugitives she was helping. Once they went with her, she was determined that they would not turn back. "You'll be free or die," she told them.[6]

Tubman's great frustration was the fatalism that plagued the people she was trying to help. Not knowing what they could be or should be, many slaves did not resist their chains. "I saved a thousand slaves," Tubman is reported to have said. "I could have saved a thousand more if only they knew they were slaves."[7]

There is a place for holy anger. We feel it for those who suffer, by their own hands or by the hands of others. When we are the ones suffering, we need anger all the more. But Job and the Canaanite woman went beyond anger. They took the audacious step of confronting God face-to-face. They crossed boundaries. They sought grace. Like Jacob at the Jabbok River, they wrestled for a blessing.

5. Hope

(or *The End of the World as We Know It*)

To put the matter starkly, nature is a cycle of sacrifice, and religion has often been no more than an attempt to reconcile us to this reality.

—David Bentley Hart[1]

The Afterlife of "Hard Times"

The curious history of Stephen Foster's song "Hard Times" involves a long period of dormancy. Following his death in 1864, many of his songs remained very popular. "Beautiful Dreamer," the last masterwork of his career, even became something of a posthumous hit, only reaching a large audience in the 1930s. But "Hard Times" was not often reprinted.

During the Great Depression, many of Foster's songs experienced a revival of popularity. Radio stations were eager to have material, and singers recorded many versions of songs such as "Jeanie with the Light Brown Hair" and "My Old Kentucky Home." The philanthropic Lilly family set out to put sheet music of Foster's songs in libraries across the country, increasing its availability. The film composer Max Steiner drew liberally from this collection in arranging music for the 1939 epic *Gone with the Wind.*[2]

"Hard Times" seems a natural fit for the Depression period, but it was not one of the tunes used by Steiner, and it was not widely recorded. Its revival had to wait for another era of dislocation—the 1970s, when a recording by the Red Clay Ramblers seems to have brought the song back to life. It has remained the most widely recorded Foster song of modern times, with numerous renditions from the likes of Willie Nelson, Yo-Yo Ma, and Nanci Griffith.[3]

What accounts for its new life in a new era? Folk artists have picked up on the simplicity and authenticity of the song, seeing it as a fitting representative of the folk tradition. But the song is flexible enough that it can be adapted for other genres as well. Recently it has once again become an anthem for difficult economic times, when the rocker Bruce Springsteen used it as a staple of his playlist during a 2009 tour. In Springsteen's hands the song became more defiant, with audiences joining him on the repeated line "Hard times, come again no more" to become a group protest against the darkness of the days.[4] Then in 2010 Mary J. Blige gave the song a gospel feel, as she recorded it for a relief album in the wake of the Haiti earthquake.[5]

Foster touched some bedrock of human experience in "Hard Times" that moves it beyond the sentimentality and wistfulness that sometimes overwhelm his other songs. "Hard Times" is about the drama of human life lived out against the backdrop of forces beyond our control. At the same time it gives dignity to individual struggles and to the cry against those forces. These have been powerful, poignant themes ever since the 1850s, but in the globalized world of the twenty-first century they have found new resonance. We all want to know what sort of world this is and how we can respond when it threatens to dehumanize us.

Providence

Ultimately, hard times lead us to consider the nature of this world, a subject that theology has traditionally addressed in its doctrine of Providence. Providence deals with the care that God takes for the world and the ways that God is involved in it to bring about the Reign of God. In dealing unflinchingly with life's hard times, we introduce a force that troubles God's relationship with the world. We also make a statement about the world that assumes our struggles in it have meaning. There is something at stake in these struggles. We are railing against hard times because there is something to confront.

This way of talking can make people nervous, especially within the realm of Christian theology. Many heirs of the sixteenth-century reformer John Calvin are hesitant to grant hard times much independent reality at all. If God is sovereign and Lord of all, as Calvin affirmed before all else, then how can we say there are forces at work in the universe that are not God-directed? God has ordered this world in all its glory and all things serve God, even when they do not seem to be good for us. God has determined the course of history, such that even an economic meltdown or a tragic death ultimately works toward the glory of God. So goes the argument.

Defending God's sovereignty in this way against the challenge of suffering often leads to grand portraits of the universe where each of the interlocking parts may seem heartless but the overall scheme is masterful. The death of a child appears senseless in isolation, but as a part of some grand design that is invisible to us, that death finds its place in the wonder of creation. This line of thinking can result in the well-intended cruelty that is inflicted on a grieving family when someone says, "God must have needed another flower for his garden." What sort of heavenly garden requires an earthly zone of woe to provide its stock?

Much as Job's outrage creeps into my thinking when I consider such a question, I recognize here the attempt to provide a faithful witness to the God of Israel and Jesus Christ. When the psalmist declares, "In your book were written / all the days that were formed for me, / when none of them as yet existed" (Psalm 139:16), there is a trust that all my days exist within God's designs. When Jesus affirms that "even the hairs of your head are all counted" (Luke 12:7), there is an implicit faith that not even so small a thing as a plucked hair is outside God's purposes.

Yet when we say that God's control over the universe includes the things that assail us, we suddenly lose the drama of creation. In fact, we may lose creation itself as a realm set apart by God with its own freedom. If every small act, good or evil, has been scripted by the will of God, then, as David Bentley Hart says, "everything is merely a fragment of divine volition, and God is simply the totality of all that is and all that happens."[6] The kingdom has come, and there is no point to calling the end of days a restoration, because nothing has ever really been lost. This vision of the world is mere determinism, with no room for contingency and real freedom. There is not much at stake in our day-to-day struggles, because somehow it is all part of the plan.

Evil

Evil is not so easily assimilated into Christian theology. Even John Calvin would not ascribe it to God. It remains out there as something God does not will and does not do. But if God is not responsible for it, where does it come from, especially given that God is the creator of all that is?

In the book of Job this is a contested question. The first two chapters of the story depict a heavenly court where the evil that befalls Job results from a more general discussion of the potential of human beings to do good and to be righteous. The Satan is not the embodiment of evil in this scene. He has a role within the heavenly realm, and he is carrying it out by proposing the test of Job. If there is evil here, from heaven's perspective, it is only because Job cannot perceive his role in a drama that is ultimately about his capacity for fidelity to God. Or, to use the language of God and Job's wife, it is about whether he will maintain his integrity as a God-fearing, evil-shunning Israelite.

However, the straightforward setup of the opening chapters soon gives way to a more complex vision of evil and the world. Once we descend to the human plane, there are chapters of agonizing over the source of Job's sufferings. In various ways Job's friends try to protect a moral universe in which God rejects evil by punishing the one who does evil. Job or his family must be the problem, according to this line of thought, despite his protestations of uprightness.

Job, on the other hand, is incensed by the injustice of it all and seeks God out as an ally. Even though in his turmoil he feels that God has turned against him, he holds out hope that an avenger will come and that he will once again see God on his side (Job 19:25-27). For Job, evil may have come from the action of God, but ultimately it is alien to God's character. God, in the end, brings vindication over evil.

God of the Whirlwind

God's confrontation with Job at the end of the book, however, is not exactly a direct confirmation of Job's convictions. God shows up in chapter 38. Right after one of Job's friends has made another speech saying that mortals cannot find God, there is God speaking from a whirlwind, and God is angry, mocking. "Who is this who obscures my intentions with his ignorant words?" asks

God. "Stand up and answer like a man" (Job 38:2-3 author's translation).

Then for four chapters God goes on to ask Job questions. "Where were you when I laid the foundations of the earth? Can you send rain on the earth? Do you know when the mountain goats give birth? Do you set the wild donkeys free? Can you comprehend the wonder of my creatures?" On and on God goes, describing the teeming creation and demanding a response from Job.

It is an impressive display, but it has struck many readers through the years as beside the point. As the Old Testament scholar John Holbert observes, "Job talks about justice and God talks about ostriches. Isn't that a non-sequitur?"[7] But Job does not seem to be confused by God. When he finally speaks, he is humbled. "I have spoken about what I didn't understand," he says. "Things too wonderful for me, which I didn't know. . . . I am cast down like trash and repent in dust and ashes." That's it.

Why is Job content with this? Why does Job let God get away without an explanation? Maybe it is because there is no answer that can satisfy the person for whom the whole world comes down to "what happens to me." There will always be some injustice to the world from my perspective. If God made it so that I would never suffer cancer, my hangnail would rise to the level of an existential question. If I never suffered grief, then the guy cutting me off on the road would make me question God's goodness. There will always be something.

Or perhaps Job is content because he hears in God's soliloquy an invitation to a new relationship with the world and with suffering. We are rightly impressed with God's thunderous display. The sheer magnitude of the volley reminds us that "the problems of three little people [let alone one] don't amount to a hill of beans in this crazy world," to quote Humphrey Bogart's character in Casablanca.[8] But it is the craziness of this world that is striking.

God is not just giving Job a show of force. Embedded in the bombast is an intricate description of a creation God does care about in intimate detail. It is a world of which humans are just a part and in which chaos and death are forever entwined with life and order. In his book *The Comforting Whirlwind: God, Job and the Scale of Creation*, Bill McKibben marvels that God, in this speech, celebrates not only the beautiful but "the disgusting." One of the creatures God lifts up is the vulture (an eagle in many translations) that "makes its nest on high" and whose "young ones suck up blood; / and where the slain are, there it is" (Job 39:27-30). "Job complains the world makes no sense and God shows him the little vultures drinking blood," McKibben says. God reveals a wild world in which suffering occurs. But "wildness is such a gift, a gift worth suffering for."[9]

Holbert concludes from this speech that God is not just chiding Job into submission. The Author of the Universe is still authoring in the face of a "tough, deadly, rapacious, blood-thirsty wildness." Chaos and evil, represented by Behemoth and Leviathan in God's soliloquy, are yet to be contained and defeated.[10] McKibben says, "It is not a storybook we were born into, but a rich and complicated novel without any conclusion. Every page of this novel sparks of delight—not rational, painless, comfortable, easy pleasure, but delight."[11] God challenges Job to be a fellow-struggler, a co-conspirator with God in the divine action of bringing all things within the orbit of God's reign. And perhaps Job will also taste some of the majestic joy God takes in this wild creation.

"This Is the Big Time Here, Every Minute of It"

The quotation at the beginning of this chapter points to a worrying tendency within religion. In the effort to protect God from blame, we will sometimes deny what is right in front of us or content ourselves with the belief that suffering is acceptable because it is natural. Hart's point, however, is that the Christian message ought to lead us to say that something is fundamentally askew in the world as it is. The glory of God "renders the very category of 'nature' mysterious, alters it, elevates it—judges and redeems it."[12]

Annie Dillard's brief essay "A Deer in Providencia" draws us to the heart of the issue. The deer in question is an animal tied to a tree with a rope around its neck. Dillard and three North American companions encountered the deer as they visited an Ecuadorian jungle village. The deer struggled fiercely against its bonds but only managed to increase its misery by getting three of its legs entangled in the rope. "Repeatedly the deer paused, motionless, its eyes veiled, with only its rib cage in motion, and its breaths the only sound," Dillard says. "Then, after I would think, 'It has given up; now it will die,' it would heave."

The party went on to have a wonderful lunch during which they could still see the deer and its suffering. They ate deer meat, which, Dillard notes, was tender because "high levels of lactic acid, which builds up in muscle tissues during exertion, tenderize." When they finished lunch, they walked around the deer to return to the boats on which they traveled. The one unavoidable thing in the village, whose English name is Providence, was the obvious trauma experienced by this deer.

Dillard says that later that night her companions, all "metropolitan men" from North America, quizzed her about her reactions to the animal. "Gentlemen of the city," she asks, "what surprises you? That there is suffering here, or that I know it?"[13] They go on to tell her that their wives would have been scandalized by the deer's plight and would have felt compelled to free it.

The implication here is that one of the intentions of civilization—understood as the whole construct of human society, intellectual and physical—is to shield us (and perhaps women in particular) from the reality of suffering. But anyone with eyes can see what's really going on. There is always a deer in the middle of the village. There is always evil in the midst of Providence, even in suburbia. The challenge is for us to see it and still go on.

Dillard concludes the essay with a description of her morning routine. Each day she rises and looks in her mirror, on which she has posted a newspaper photo of a man wrapped in bandages who had been horribly burned for the second time in his life. Accompanying the photo is a quote from the man asking why God would do this to him a second time. Though she doesn't explain the meaning of this routine, it suggests that the only way truly to live in this world is to look deeply into its suffering and to choose to go on. "This is the Big Time here," Dillard says, "every minute of it."[14]

Dillard's newspaper clipping may sound, at the least, eccentric, but Christians have meditated on suffering as a spiritual practice for centuries. What is the crucifix on the walls and jewelry of so many Roman Catholic Christians except a visual reminder of the centrality of suffering in our primary story? And more than a reminder: an invitation into a great mystery.

The Glass Coffin

In the main cathedral of the Mexican city of Puebla there is a glass coffin. I came to the church in the midst of a trip through southern Mexico to catalog needs that might be addressed by future work teams from churches in the United States. I visited remote villages with few modern services. I went to urban centers where old buildings were falling into disrepair. I spent time at an orphanage where one woman and her two teenage daughters were providing a home for up to forty children, sometimes with so few resources that they went weeks at a time with no basics such as milk. Then I came to the glass coffin.

The cathedral in Puebla is grand, in the Spanish colonial style. Its twin towers are the highest in Mexico. It has a magnificent choir in the chancel with inlaid wood of eight different colors. Its interior space soars to the heavens. But the glass coffin is the most affecting sight in the building.

Located near the main entrance, it contains a near-life-size wooden sculpture of the crucified Jesus as he lay in the tomb. There is, however, no calm repose or ease in this Jesus. The haunting grace of a traditional Pietà with Jesus draped across the lap of his mother is not to be found here. This Jesus, like the wood from which he is carved, is knotted and twisted. The most remarkable thing about him is his woundedness. The pain that he bore is still evident as he lies in the grave.

The coffin caught me by surprise as I walked around the nave of the cathedral. It was so horrific that I felt a need to turn my eyes away, but I could not. This Jesus was truly incarnate. Irretrievably embodied. His suffering was no illusion. He came to share the life of those who carried on their struggle with hard times in dusty desert towns and bare, bereft orphanages. The broken Christ reveals that the point at which the world seems to make the least sense—in its trauma and pain—is the very point where God makes a stand and declares who God is: a God who stood beside the broken Israel and who stands with the broken of every place.

Near the cathedral is the Santo Domingo Church, another colonial-era building that features a brilliant Baroque chapel made of gilded stucco and onyx. Gold glitters from every surface. But beneath all the gold is a history of suffering that was once embodied in all the indigenous laborers who worked to mine the riches that are now so extravagantly displayed. The intent may be to glorify Jesus, but the solidarity he displayed with suffering humanity is on view in the glass coffin on a side aisle at the cathedral.

The Empty-Tomb Ending

Any theology that turns us away from the crucified Christ cannot deal realistically with evil. For Christians this is the compelling image from which we cannot avert our gaze. It is the radical stance of God in the world that changes our perception of how God meets hard times and how God deals with them. In Jesus, God is revealed as the One who meets suffering by entering it, enduring it, and ultimately triumphing over it.

Jesus does not show an easy acceptance of evil. In fact, he rebukes demons and casts out darkness. But he plays by an alternate set of rules, because he does not accept the notion that evil has a claim on him. Evil may mar, deface, and deform the good, but it cannot define the world that God has created. The character of the world is forever marked by redemption as shown in Jesus on the cross.

The early church leader Augustine of Hippo was influential in developing a vocabulary for talking about evil. Augustine thought of evil not as a thing in itself but rather as the privation of good. Evil has no existence in the sense that we talk about created things existing. Since God did not give it being, it is a shadow representing that which God did not intend. And though it is not intended, we nevertheless find it within our lives and in the world.

This way of talking seems preposterous at first blush. How can we say that evil doesn't exist when it manifestly does have real influence on the world? It's no comfort to Job to say that evil doesn't really exist. But on further examination, as we try to locate evil, Augustine's view begins to make sense. Where did the evil of the Holocaust come from? Was it incarnate in those who perpetrated it, and therefore what sort of people were they? Were they of a different species from us? Or were they very much like us—prone to sin and error and influenced by any number of factors yet also created by God for good? Was evil in the ideologies of racial superiority or the legacy of anti-Semitism? Was it in some alien force that overtook them? The evil was obvious and widespread, yet its source is elusive.

We also don't want to say that because evil has no created reality it therefore is not our concern. It is ever our concern. Karl Barth, the twentieth-century theologian, said that "if being is to be ascribed to [evil] at all, and we would rather not say that it is non-existent, then it is only the power of being that arises from the divine 'No.' "[15] That is to say, evil rises to the level of our awareness because God has rejected it. God takes it seriously but does not affirm it. Therefore, we also must take it seriously but ought not give it more power or reality than it has in God's eyes. The end of the world as we know it, its purpose and meaning, is not bound up in nihilism and death. The end is an empty tomb.

6. Beauty and Joy

(or After the Storm)

O LORD, my heart is not lifted up,
my eyes are not raised too high;
I do not occupy myself with things
too great and too marvelous for me.
But I have calmed and quieted my soul,
like a weaned child with its mother;
my soul is like the weaned child that is with me.

O Israel, hope in the LORD
from this time on and forevermore.

—PSALM 131

"I know that you can do all things,
and that no purpose of yours can be thwarted.
'Who is this that hides counsel without knowledge?'
Therefore I have uttered what I did not understand,
things too wonderful for me, which I did not know."

—JOB 42:2-3

If I truly heeded the wisdom in these two biblical passages, this chapter would probably not be written. Perhaps this book would not be written. Certainly the meaning of suffering is

73

one of those things "too great and too marvelous for me," and I have often "uttered what I did not understand." But having come this far, I tread forward with humility and caution, reminding the reader once more that this is not the last word on a perpetual mystery at the heart of the universe. It is merely another report from a wondering witness.

How to conclude a reflection on hard times? If you treat this book like a mystery novel and flip to the final chapter to get the answer to life's most persistent questions, you will be disappointed. Eugene Rogers, one of my former professors, who has thought deeply about these things, says that one of the things that makes evil evil is that it does not make sense. It resists answers and comprehensive definitions. If it could be brought within the bounds of our reason, it would not be so . . . evil. So answers here would be problematic.

If not answers, perhaps we can mark out stances, postures, convictions that may put us in a position to hear some new word from God. We are, after all, children in this journey. I aspire to be like the weaned child of Psalm 131—hopeful, quieted, and anticipating more growth. So what follows is not so much lessons learned as it is preliminary presumptions on the way to childhood.

The Last Days of Foster and Job

Our primary companions in this exploration of hard times have been an unlikely pair: a formerly rich man on an ash heap and a gifted composer whose life was marked by trials. The stories of Job and Stephen Foster could not have come to more different ends. Foster died in sad circumstances. Faint from fever, he fell in his small Bowery hotel room and received a fatal gash in his neck as he hit the bed stand. His few possessions included thirty-eight cents and a small slip of paper on which he had written the words "Dear friends and gentle hearts."[1] This incomplete sentence recalls the deep longings of his best music.

The final verse of "Hard Times Come Again No More" seems to capture Foster's conception of death. The end is stark with a "lowly grave" around which mourners gather. All that remains of life is the sigh, the wail, the dirge that carries on even after death: "Hard times, come again no more."

Job has a much more surprising conclusion. After the devastation, after the loss, after the cries to heaven and the fruitless rationalization of the friends, after the storm in which God appears to him and the final repentance of Job in dust and ashes—what happens then?

Job is restored—at least, as much as is possible. God gives Job twice as much as he had before. He had 7,000 sheep; now he has 14,000. He had 3,000 camels before, 6,000 after; 500 yoke of oxen, now 1,000; 500 donkeys, now 1,000. His brothers and sisters and all who had known him before come over to break bread with him. He has seven more sons and three more daughters. He lives for 140 more years and sees his children and his children's children and their children too.

Of all the things that happen in the book of Job, I think this conclusion is the most disturbing. It seems to say that if we just endure, God will bless us with every material blessing. If we just hold on and stay faithful, no matter what the Satan can throw at us, we will have 1,000 donkeys! But this is not so. We have seen faithful people, saints even, endure unimaginable things, and they never receive their long life and riches. If we assume that Job's restoration is the norm for all the faithful who endure suffering, we will be disillusioned. So what shall we do with hard times?

1. *Trust in the words and deeds that make Christians distinctive.*

There is something to be said for committing ourselves to things we hope we believe. Marriage is one of those things. I have had the privilege of being a part of many services of Christian marriage, and it never ceases to amaze me that otherwise level-headed people will take on vows the meaning of which they have no way of conceiving. What outrageous folly! To pledge yourself to another person for better or worse? Do we imagine that worse will only mean cold feet and snoring in bed? No, it could mean caring for your partner through strokes or cancer. It could mean struggling together through addictions. What heartbreak we lay ourselves open for when we say those words!

The words enact the marriage, though. We say them despite our ignorance, and if we are fortunate we learn what marriage is by living into the words. It may be that none of us is truly capable of the radical commitment embodied in marriage, but we trust the words and we trust the God whom we invite to be a witness and a party to the pledge.

The liturgy of the Christian community has often been a comfort to me in times of grief and struggle. Throughout my life I have been prone to depression, one of the most debilitating features of which is an inability to derive pleasure from the things that have been vital to my soul. At its worst, depression left me sitting on the floor staring at a blank wall, trying to recover some spark that would get me, if not back to life, at least out the door and into the world. During these periods it was often the words of the familiar church services that carried me until the sap in my veins began to flow once more.

Like the friends who brought a paralyzed man to Jesus and lowered him through a roof so that he could be healed, the words of the church have often borne me back to life. And still, when the gathered group at a funeral begins the recitation of the Twenty-third Psalm, I am aware that there is some steady current moving us along toward God, even when we cannot muster trust in the resurrection that we confess. It is important to say the words.

Lauren Winner, in her book *Mudhouse Sabbath: An Invitation to Spiritual Discipline,* writes about an experience of sitting next to her boyfriend's grandfather, Dr. Gatewood, during a church service. Suffering from some loss of memory, Dr. Gatewood is often not coherent, but on this occasion Winner notices that he is able to recite every word of the Lord's Prayer and the Apostle's Creed. "What I know is this," she says. "Those words of prayer are the most basic words Dr. Gatewood knows. When he has forgotten everything else, those words are the words he will have. Those words have formed his heart, and—regardless of what he feels or remembers on any particular morning—they continue to form his heart still."[2]

There is a similar disorientation that we experience when hard times come our way. We wonder if the ground has forever shifted beneath our feet. We are aware of our vulnerability and our utter dependency on other people and events beyond our control. The labor of Christians is to look upon the words and practices that have formed us, trusting that they will lead us to a new day beyond the darkness.

2. Cultivate the restless desire that points us toward our ultimate end.

I am not a visual artist, but I have come to appreciate the way art can do an end-run around the cognitive brain to reveal truth. As a result, on all-too-rare occasions, I have dabbled in some art project with skills that have not improved much since the third grade. One such instance was on a retreat with a group of college students. The assignment was broad and not one that I remember. Whatever it was, I used the opportunity to express the way I was feeling at the time and, because my analytical side would not shut down entirely, to depict what it meant to be human. No small task.

Using glue, tissue paper, and construction paper, we all set to work. I chose black as the background color—the darkness of night and mystery—and brown for the ground across the bottom. The rest was crude hands and feet, arranged in such a way that they suggested a body teetering and about to fall. Only one foot touched the ground. The other was raised into the air, where it was being touched by Michelangelo's God from the Sistine Chapel (or at least my facsimile of the same). A cross stood in the center of the undrawn body, a nod to Colossians 3:3—"Your life is hidden with Christ in God." And streaming through the space where a body should have been, there were streaks of red tissue paper representing fire, passion, the Holy Spirit.

God's finger touching the foot was just me being cheeky. The Adam of the Sistine Chapel looks far too composed to be the kind of human I feel like most days. Better that God should be authoring a human being all akimbo.

The cross at the center was a reflection of some theological study I was doing at the time. Under the influence of the theologian Karl Barth I began to see Jesus everywhere, even in the formation of human identity. Once identified as the incarnate God, Jesus reveals the intentions of God for every individual and the shape of true humanity.

The streams of red, though, were the key to it all. If there is one enduring constant in my experience of life, it has been the restless movement of my soul toward God. When I am attentive to that drumbeat, I am alive. When I neglect it, I wither. Always it is a holy discomfort. *Sehnsucht* might be an apt description for this longing. It provides the context for the incompleteness and brokenness we experience in this life. We are always en route, as individuals and as peoples.

3. Recall that victory is not a human capacity but a divine assurance.

It is presumptuous to suggest that we can experience victory over suffering, because it implies that the victory is achievable by sheer force of will and individual effort. The phrase suggests a title for the self-help section of the bookstore, where it would join books that promise better bodies and better relationships in ten easy steps.

Victory, in this case, is not something human beings can achieve. We have all heard stories of people who come through struggles with hard times and who claim that it was the best thing that ever happened to them. There is a whole culture of folks who say that their cancer, their horrible divorce, their lost job *saved* them. By that they must mean that they discovered some life-giving lesson in the midst of the darkness, like my colleague who sometimes looks back with nostalgia on the time when she broke her ankle because it taught her to slow down and depend on others.

These revelations, however, are not the same thing as victories. They are silver linings in the cloud or the opportunity edge of a crisis, not testimonies to where our hope ultimately lies. Sometimes we cannot transform bad things into good things. Sometimes we cannot overcome evil with the best of our efforts and positive thinking. At some point we have to trust that victory is a promise within which we live our lives. It is the assurance offered by the Easter light already shining into the Good Friday world. Ultimately, it is grace.

It takes a believer to see through to this victory by grace. It takes a believer to see how something as empty as a tomb can change the world. To quote once more from David Bentley Hart: "When . . . we learn in Christ the nature of our first estate, and the divine destiny to which we are called, we begin to see—more clearly the more we are able to look upon the world with the eye of charity—that there is in all the things of earth a hidden glory waiting to be revealed, more radiant than a million suns, more beautiful than the most generous imagination or most ardent desire can now conceive."[3]

4. *We are not only victims but agents who can address suffering where we can.*

Trusting in a victory that ultimately is not ours, however, is not an excuse for passivity in the face of injustice and trial. If Job and the Canaanite woman teach anything, it is that there is dignity in the sufferer that demands a hearing. Accepting a title of victim is just one more way in which those who suffer disappear behind a generality.

When we lose our sense of agency, we begin to thin, to lose our substance, to become the "frail forms fainting at the door." We start to accept that the way things are is the way they were meant to be, and we toss only half-hearted rebukes to the hard times that come to call. "Save us from weak resignation to the evils we deplore," declares Harry Emerson Fosdick's hymn, "God of Grace and God of Glory."[4]

Scott Cairns in *The End of Suffering* says, "The very heart of an efficacious faith, it seems to me now, is bound up precisely in our—watchfully—living into this mystery of what appears to be God's continuing desire for collaboration between Himself and His creation."[5] Despite all the real risks that are entailed and all the errors and horrors that sometimes ensue, God seeks partners and invites us (even us!) into the struggle with hard times.

My friend Juan Prieto is someone who has often moved me to claim the possibilities of partnership. We first met when we were both working with youth in the neighborhoods of inner-city Dallas, Texas. I was the new youth director for a community center, and Juan worked with the city health department. For some reason I came into my role with the illusion that there would be elders, experts who could confidently guide me in addressing the needs of that troubled community. To be fair, there were some who brought wisdom and experience to their roles. But urban community work is hard, and long tenures are the exception. In addition, the problems are often overwhelming.

When I began to despair over making a difference, it was Juan who helped me see the possibilities. With a prophet's vision, Juan could imagine how things might be if we nurtured them. Together we worked on creating a Teen Advisory Council to allow youth themselves to be involved in changing things. The most visible fruit of that effort was a talent show that featured thirty-four rap acts and one magical Latin dance. Gradually I began to see that we were becoming the very people I had hoped to find. While neither Juan nor I would have claimed to be experts, we discovered the freedom to act and to work toward a community where everyone was engaged in the fight against hard times. Juan, I'm happy to say, is still creating environments where change can happen.

5. Do not neglect to see beauty.

If there is one core belief that has animated the writing of this book, it is that beauty is the sustaining feature of the universe. This world is fierce and vast and devastating, but above all it is beautiful and God is everywhere within. This is why a figure like Stephen Foster, who makes such a poor Sunday school exemplar, speaks to me. He was captivated by visions of a world where everyone found the home they were searching for. His music played to the sentiments of people whose lives were disrupted in many different ways. Even in his failings there are moments of heartbreaking beauty. So Foster, like every human person when viewed through the lens of God's love, is finally revealed to be a bearer of light.

The same is true of the smallest created thing. Once I tried to discern the light in a magnolia tree out my window. It was a scraggly tree hidden among other scraggly trees near a small creek. By the time I had spent ten minutes writing about the tree, I was convinced that it contained the universe. I know now that if that tree falls before I do, I will mourn its loss. Even that magnolia is filled with the glory of God. I trust that God sees in each one of us a little bit of that wonder.

My friend Lisa Stevens Powers is a folk singer who moonlights as a midwife. She introduced me to a song by Cheryl Wheeler called "Little Road," which is a bittersweet celebration of the small things in this life. Lisa discovered it during a time when she was facing hard times:

> I was working in a practice in Lenoir, North Carolina. The community had been hit hard by the recession and most of my patients were out of work and not likely to find work any time in the foreseeable future. . . . I was going to work every day and I was surrounded by anger. I was cursed at and yelled at on a regular basis. I had no control over the schedule and no control over my life. I felt so very, very hopeless. . . . I didn't know what I was going to do. And every day felt like it was the last day I could take it.
>
> I was driving around in my car when I heard [this] song for the first time. . . . I was crying inside. That kind of crying that you do when depression is so heavy on your heart that your tears are all dried up and all the crying is inside of yourself, with no way out. It was a cold, crystal clear winter day. The bluest skies are in the winter like that. Deep, clear endless blue. And I could see Grandfather Mountain, covered in snow, off in the distance, in all that blue. And "Little Road" came on. And Grandfather was so beauti-

ful. And it was as if God had spoken clearly to me, "People are not easy. Work is hard. But you have everything you need to do it and you have relief from it because there is beauty. Just look."

Cheryl was singing about how she "just looked" [and saw] the little road that winds along the river. When she sang the two lines about "and a father hugs his daughter / and an old man holds the car door for his wife to come and see / then they turn at smile at me / how can there be such trouble in this world?," it was like a dam broke inside of me and I was set loose. I knew it wasn't going to be easy but that the world is not terrible.[6]

Lisa writes songs like that too, and because she does I know that the world is not terrible but awesome and fiercely beautiful.

6. Trust the joy.

The resurrection confidence of Christians is that love ultimately wins the day. Perhaps our greatest weapon, then, in facing down suffering is joy. Joy seems rather insubstantial and maybe even frivolous when faced with the seriousness of hard times. But joy is not the talent of being oblivious to the obvious, ignoring the reality of pain. Instead, it is the capacity to see through the struggles to a larger, redeemed reality.

Barbara Tankard, to whom this book is dedicated, had this kind of joy. I only got to know her late in her life as she was battling recurring cancer. Her last year was particularly difficult as she survived life-threatening surgery only to be felled by the cancer a few months later. She was surrounded to the end by dedicated friends who had walked with her through many trials, including the death of her husband a few years before.

What defined Barbara, however, was not the extent of her trials but the cockeyed pleasure she found in impermanent things. She was prone to all-night scrapbooking parties, not so much for what was produced but for the giddy intimacy with her companions. Once she dressed as a lion to crawl around the stage at a talent show with children who were as close to her as if she had adopted them. There was nothing but joy on her face that night. Barbara took immense joy in things that do not last—the company of friends and family, the wonder of a small child destined to grow up, deep laughter, a heartfelt performance, good music, a well-cooked meal, a dance, a prayer. All these things come and go, most leaving no lasting trace, but she savored them all.

Was Barbara Tankard insufficiently aware of her condition? Did she not know the injustice of what she was going through? Shouldn't she have mustered some of Job's bluster to declare herself the wronged party in some cosmic game being played at her expense? She could have. She certainly had every right to feel aggrieved. If she had counted her dedication to God in a system of rewards, she might well have asked, "Is this what all my faithfulness has bought me?"

She didn't think about her faith that way, though. Or if she did, she kept it far from the sight of those who knew her. Instead she knew the desire Stephen Foster talks about: to "seek mirth and beauty and music light and gay." It was the beauty and the joy, fierce joy, that captivated her, and these seem far better categories for truth than reason ever has been. If this is true, then one of the primary duties of Christians is to try and pattern their lives after the glory they glimpse in the Bible and in their visions of heaven.

Christian writers through the ages have sometimes used musical terms to talk about this struggle. Saint Ambrose said, "Just as our hope is in a perfect octave, so that octave is our highest virtuous efforts."[7] In other words, when we live just right, when we love just right, when we do justice, when we love kindness, the note we ring vibrates in sympathy with its octave note in heaven. There is a correspondence between this life and the next when we discover the kingdom of heaven at hand among us already.

Our songs of deepest love and profoundest joy can be sung in minor keys. While life persists in this earthly realm, so will hard times. But Barbara and all the saints who have fought back against suffering with a deep and radical joy look forward to a new day when the "song, the sigh of the weary" is sung in the aftermath of victory, and hard times will come again no more.

NOTES

Introduction

1. Rabindranath Tagore, ThinkExist.com, http://thinkexist.com/ quotation/faith_is_the_bird_that_feels_the_light_and_sings/14481.html.

1. Spirit

1. Gerard Manley Hopkins, "I Wake and Feel," in *Hopkins: Poems and Prose,* Everyman's Library Pocket Poets, (New York: Alfred A. Knopf, 1995), p. 71.

2. "The American Experience: Stephen Foster," PBS television movie, transcript, http://www.pbs.org/wgbh/amex/foster/filmmore/index.html.

3. "While the Bowl Goes Round," words by George Cooper, music by Stephen Foster, in Steven Saunders and Deane L. Root, *The Music of Stephen C. Foster,* vol. 2 (Washington: Smithsonian Institution Press, 1990), pp. 276–78.

4. "The Last Years of Stephen Foster," originally appeared in "The New York Clipper," March 1877, found in "Foster Hall Bulletin," No. 10, May 1934, p. 5. In the collection at the Stephen Foster Collection, University of Pittsburgh.

5. Ibid.

6. "The Girl Who Can't Feel Pain: Rare Disorder Affects Ability to Tell Whether She Is Harming Herself," Good Morning America website, ABC News, December 9, 2005, http://abcnews.go.com/GMA/OnCall/story?id=1386322 (accessed on October 9, 2009).

7. Ian Urbina, "An Old World Close to a New World Horror," *The New York Times*, October 6, 2006, http://www.nytimes.com/2006/10/06/us/06amish.html (accessed February 19, 2010).

8. David Bentley Hart, *The Doors of the Sea* (Grand Rapids, Mich.: Eerdmans, 2005), p. 58.

2. Longing

1. Stephen Foster, "My Old Kentucky Home, Good Night" (1853).

2. Stephen Foster's sketchbook in the Foster Hall Collection, Center for American Music, University of Pittsburgh Library System, p. 55 recto, entry dated June 26, 1851.

3. Stephen Foster, "Poor Drooping Maiden," prepared by Steven Saunders and Deane L. Root, *The Music of Stephen C. Foster*, vol. 2 (Washington: Smithsonian Institution Press, 1990), pp. 82–84. Original date, 1860.

4. Dr. Deane L. Root, Director, Center for American Music, University of Pittsburgh, interview with the author, February 13, 2009, transcription 2, p. 4. Referred to hereafter as Root.

5. Root, transcription 1, p. 8.

6. Deane Root in "Stephen Foster," PBS film in the American Experience series, transcript at http://www.pbs.org/wgbh/amex/foster/filmmore/pt.html. Referred to hereafter as PBS.

7. PBS, Ken Emerson.

8. Dr. Edward Ayers, President, University of Richmond, interview with the author, February 15, 2010, transcription, p. 2.

9. Stephen Foster, "Old Folks at Home," lyrics at http://www.poemhunter.com/poem/old-folks-at-home/.

10. Stephen Foster, "Stephen Foster Lyrics" at http://www.pitt.edu/~amerimus/lyrics.htm. Foster Hall Collection, Center for American Music, University of Pittsburgh Library System.

11. Root, transcription 1, p. 9.

12. D. G. Kehl, "Writing the Long Desire: The Function of *Sehnsucht* in *The Great Gatsby* and *Look Homeward, Angel,*" *Journal of Modern Lit-*

erature, December 22, 2000, http://www.accessmylibrary.com/article -1G1-80682150/writing-long-desire-function.html.

13. William Safire, "Hard Times," *The New York Times Magazine,* February 19, 2009, http://www.nytimes.com/2009/02/22/maga zine/22wwln-safire-t.html?_r=2.

14. George W. Birdseye, "Sketch of the Late Stephen C. Foster," originally appeared in the *N.Y. Musical Gazette,* reprinted in *Western Musical World,* Cleveland, Vol. IV, No. 1, January 1867, p. 3. Referred to hereafter as Birdseye.

15. PBS, Deane Root.

16. "Timeline," on PBS-TV site for "Stephen Foster," PBS film in the American Experience series. http://www.pbs.org/wgbh/amex/ foster/timeline/timeline2.html.

17. Ibid.

18. "The Last Years of Stephen Foster," originally appeared in "The New York Clipper," March 1877, found in "Foster Hall Bulletin," No. 10, May 1934, p. 2. In the collection at the Stephen Foster Collection, University of Pittsburgh.

19. Birdseye, p. 3.

20. Ibid.

21. Steven Saunders and Deane L. Root, *The Music of Stephen C. Foster,* vol. 2 (Washington: Smithsonian Institution Press, 1990), pp. 172-74.

22. Ibid., pp. 380-82.

23. MS letter from Henrietta A. Thornton to brother, Morrison Foster, June 10, 1859, in the Foster Hall Collection, Center for American Music, University of Pittsburgh.

24. Samuel J. Rogal, "The Gospel Hymns of Stephen Collins Foster," *The Hymn* vol. 21, no. 1, January 1970 (Hymn Society of America: New York), pp. 10-11.

25. Augustine, *Confessions,* trans. F. J. Sheed (Indianapolis: Hackett Publishing Co., 1993), p. 3.

26. W. H. Lewis, ed., *Letters of C. S. Lewis* (New York: Harcourt Brace & World, 1966), 289, quoted in Terry Lindvall, "Joy and *Sehnsucht*: The Laughter and Longings of C. S. Lewis," *Mars Hill Review* 8 (Summer 1997), pp. 25-38, http://www.leaderu.com/marshill/mhr08/hall1. html#text14.

27. C. S. Lewis, *The Problem of Pain* (New York: HarperCollins e-book, 1940), locations 1640-1659.

3. Anger

1. Author's translation.

2. James 5:11 (KJV).

3. See, for example, the New Revised Standard Version and the *New American Bible*.

4. "Do Not Go Gentle into That Good Night," from *The Poems of Dylan Thomas* (New York: New Directions, 1971). Copyright © 1952, 1953 Dylan Thomas; poets.org, http://www.poets.org/viewmedia.php/prmMID/15377 (accessed February 19, 2010).

5. David Bentley Hart, *The Doors of the Sea* (Grand Rapids, Mich.: Eerdmans, 2005), pp. 85-86.

6. Scott Cairns, *The End of Suffering: Finding Purpose in Pain* (Brewster, Mass.: Paraclete Press, 2009), p. 7.

7. Josef Stalin, http://www.brainyquote.com/quotes/quotes/j/josephstal137476.html. Evidence that it may be misattributed: http://en.wikiquote.org/wiki/Joseph_Stalin.

8. Jedediah Purdy, *For Common Things: Irony, Trust, and Commitment in America Today* (New York: Vintage Books, 2000), p. 10.

4. Audacity

1. John 4:1-39.

2. Matthew 9:20-22; Mark 5:25-34; Luke 8:43-48.

3. Luke 7:36-39.

4. Gerard Manley Hopkins, "God's Grandeur," in *Hopkins: Poems and Prose*, Everyman's Library Pocket Poets (New York: Alfred A. Knopf, 1995), p. 14.

5. Job 39:1-4.

6. "Harriet Tubman," Africans in America series, PBS, http://www.pbs.org/wgbh/aia/part4/4p1535.html (accessed March 5, 2010).

7. Harriet Tubman quotes, Brainy Quotes, http://www.brainyquote.com/quotes/quotes/h/harriettub388682.html (accessed March 5, 2010).

5. Hope

1. David Bentley Hart, *The Doors of the Sea* (Grand Rapids, Mich.: Eerdmans, 2005), p. 52. Referred to hereafter as Hart.

2. Dr. Deane L. Root, Director, Center for American Music, University of Pittsburgh, interview with the author, February 13, 2009, transcription 3, p. 8.

3. Ibid., p. 10.

4. For a sample of Springsteen's treatment of the song see http://www.youtube.com/watch?v=f4UEC3ndqvc (accessed March 12, 2010).

5. Mary J. Blige on the *Hope for Haiti* album, released January 22, 2010.

6. Hart, p. 91.

7. John Holbert, "Preaching and the Creation: The Convenient Texts of Genesis and Job," Peyton Lecture, February 1, 2010, Minister's Week at Perkins School of Theology, Southern Methodist University, author's notes. Referred to hereafter as Holbert.

8. Rick, played by Humphrey Bogart in the 1942 movie *Casablanca*, http://www.imdb.com/title/tt0034583/quotes (accessed March 13, 2010).

9. Bill McKibben, *The Comforting Whirlwind: God, Job and the Scale of Creation* (Cambridge, Mass.: Cowley Publications, 2005), pp. 41-42. Referred to hereafter as McKibben.

10. Holbert.

11. McKibben, p. 43.

12. Hart, p. 54.

13. Annie Dillard, *The Annie Dillard Reader* (New York: Harper-Collins, 1994), pp. 115-19.

14. Ibid., p. 119.

15. Karl Barth, *Dogmatics in Outline* (New York: Harper & Row, 1959), p. 57.

6. Beauty and Joy

1. "Stephen Foster," PBS film in the American Experience series, transcript at http://www.pbs.org/wgbh/amex/foster/filmmore/pt.html.

2. Lauren Winner, *Mudhouse Sabbath: An Invitation to a Life of Spiritual Discipline* (Brewster, Mass.: Paraclete Press, 2007), p. 64.

3. Ibid.

4. Harry Emerson Fosdick, "God of Grace and God of Glory," 1930, lyrics at http://www.cyberhymnal.org/htm/g/o/godgrace.htm.

5. Scott Cairns, *The End of Suffering: Finding Purpose in Pain* (Brewster, Mass.: Paraclete Press, 2009), p. 105.

6. Lisa Steven Powers, e-mail correspondence with the author, March 14, 2010, used with permission.

7. *"Sicut enim spei nostrae octava perfectio est, ita octava summa virtutum est,"* Ambrose, quoted in Henri DeLubac, *Medieval Exegesis: Volume 2, The Four Senses of Scripture,* trans. by E. M. Macierowski (Grand Rapids, Mich.: Eerdmans, 2000), p. 187.

Study Guide

The questions that follow can be used in several ways. If you are reading this book on your own, they can be prompts to deeper reflection and interaction with what you are reading. They may be invitations to doing some writing of your own in a personal journal. Let them lead you into a more engaged experience with this book.

Small groups may find the questions useful for beginning discussions about the book. A leader could use them as the basis for a lesson plan with a group that is committed to reading together. If the group is reading a chapter per week, the questions could guide an hour to hour-and-a-half discussion.

If you are not involved in a small group but would like to form one, begin conversations with interested friends and encourage them to help you host a group. Some locales that are conducive to such groups may be coffee shops, churches, libraries, or community centers. Advertise the group through notices and flyers to attract others.

Whether you continue your reflection individually or with

others, try to obtain a recording of the Stephen Foster song "Hard Times Come Again No More." While it has been recorded many times in recent years, I would recommend the versions by the Red Clay Ramblers (on the album *Hard Times*), Emmylou Harris (on the album *Portraits*), and, for something completely different, Mary J. Blige (on the album *Hope for Haiti Now*). If you are a musician yourself, the sheet music is readily available. Play it!

1. Spirit (or Learning from Hard Times)

1. Which contemporary songs or types of music speak most powerfully to you? Why? What song would you turn to in the midst of hard times?

2. Read the lyrics or (better) listen to a recording of the Foster song "Hard Times Come Again No More." What feelings does it evoke? The author says "it is no anthem of faith. It is a window on the wounded soul." How do you assess the truth of that statement?

3. The author says, "Maybe it's time to listen to hard times again." Would you agree? What sorts of lessons have you learned through experiences of pain and hard times?

4. What are the ways that you have heard people answering the question of why hard times come? Why do these responses often seem inadequate?

5. The author says that a world without God is "a disenchanted world that offers no ultimate reconciliation, no comfort, and no redemption for the sufferer." How much of our struggle with suffering is really a struggle with God?

6. Reflect on a time when you felt that you were suffering because of circumstances you couldn't control. How would thinking of yourself as a pawn or "Satan's plaything" have affected your mood and your actions?

7. What does the example of Amish forgiveness suggest about possible responses to the presence of evil in the world?

8. Quoted in this chapter, David Bentley Hart says that the truth embedded in Christianity "gives rise not to optimism but to joy." What is the difference between the two? How have you experienced or seen others experience joy even in hard times?

9. The author says that hard times "may also illuminate an underlying richness and texture that pervade the world." In what ways have difficult situations helped you see these qualities in the world?

2. Longing (or A Thousand Miles from Home)

1. What might "the pale drooping maiden" represent in your life?

2. Recognizing that childhood memories can be complicated by many feelings, what are your earliest memories of a childhood home? What qualities made it feel like home? What parts of it would you like to experience again?

3. Foster found that slavery illuminated a tragic dimension to American life and individual lives. What resources did enslaved peoples in the United States draw on to confront hard times? How can these resources still be instructive?

4. Where do you see the kind of unrequited longing of Foster's music in our culture today? In your life? How does this song still resonate with the human condition?

5. How is *hard times* an accurate term for our current economic situation? What other terms might we use to describe the character of our days?

6. In what ways do Stephen Foster's struggles feel familiar to you? Describe your "cabin door" of contentment.

7. How can brokenness "unveil a holy discontent within us that seeks a hearing and a healing, and ultimately, a home"?

8. What is it that you "shall still desire" on your deathbed?

3. Anger (or "I Will Not Be Extinguished")

1. Read Job 2:8–3:13. How does Job's response to his crisis change in this excerpt? How can each response be seen as faithful?

2. What is the real error of the friends who come to visit Job? What would you have said or done if you were Job's friend?

3. Job "holds on to a belief in a universe where there is justice at work, where there is a moral center and God is in control." Do you admire Job for this conviction? Why or why not? What if God were not in control? What response would we have then to suffering?

4. Think about responses you and others have had to acts that seemed senseless—things such as the attacks of 9/11 or Hurri-

cane Katrina. How did we try to make these events make sense? Did the responses seem adequate?

5. The author describes an angry sermon he delivered at a funeral for a teenager. Why do we sometimes feel that anger is an inappropriate reaction to pain and suffering?

6. How does Jesus' story help us understand how God deals with evil?

7. How do large-scale instances of oppression make individual human beings invisible? How can those suffering keep from losing their identity and their sense that they have the capacity to do something in response?

8. An ironic stance protects us from real commitment, according to the author. How can a Job-like anger keep us engaged with God even in hard times?

4. Audacity (or The Woman Who Wouldn't Go Away)

1. Read the excerpt from Matthew out loud. What are the most surprising elements of the story?

2. Imagine yourself in the shoes of the woman arguing with Jesus for the healing of her child. What resources did she have? How did she use them?

3. How is the Canaanite woman a model for "calling out" Jesus? What does she demand?

4. How do you interpret Jesus' initial refusal to help the woman?

5. What does it mean that "God is prodigally present even in suffering"?

6. The author says that the woman calls out "the Jesus who is hope for the whole world." How can our struggles give us a larger vision of who God is?

7. How is Harriet Tubman an heir to the same audacity we see in the Canaanite woman?

8. What did Tubman mean when she said, "I could have saved a thousand more if only they knew they were slaves"? What message might this offer to people who need to confront the need for healing?

5. Hope (or The End of the World as We Know It)

1. Why do you think the song "Hard Times" is experiencing a revival in our times?

2. How is our belief in human freedom affected by the idea that God determines every event?

3. What is at stake in the story of Job? What messages does it give us about the source and nature of evil?

4. If, as Bill McKibben says, we are born into "a rich and complicated novel without any conclusion" and are invited to struggle with God against chaos and evil, is this comforting? Explain.

5. If there is "always a deer in the middle of the village . . . evil in the midst of Providence," how do we keep ourselves from seeing it? How does the culture keep us from being overcome by it?

6. What role does suffering play in the Christian story?

7. How is Christ's suffering a sign of God's solidarity with brokenness?

8. How does the notion that evil is what God didn't create help us understand its ultimate powerlessness?

6. Beauty and Joy (or After the Storm)

1. The author says Job's ending is the most disturbing part of his story. Why? Do you agree?

2. When have familiar words or rituals been a comfort to you in hard times? Why did they have that power?

3. The author gives the example of using art to uncover his own restless desire for God. What are other ways you could cultivate that desire?

4. How can we trust that, even when we can't "transform bad things into good things," there is a divine promise of ultimate victory over evil?

5. The story of Juan Prieto shows how we can confront evil through our own actions. When have you felt that you were becoming the answer to the prayer you offered? How did that happen?

6. The author declares that "Foster, like every human person when looked at through the lens of God's love, is finally revealed to be a bearer of light." Do you agree? Why or why not?

7. How does the beauty of the world speak to you of God's presence?

8. Think of someone who modeled for you the "capacity to see through [his or her] struggles to a larger, redeemed reality." Tell that person's story and give thanks for him or her.